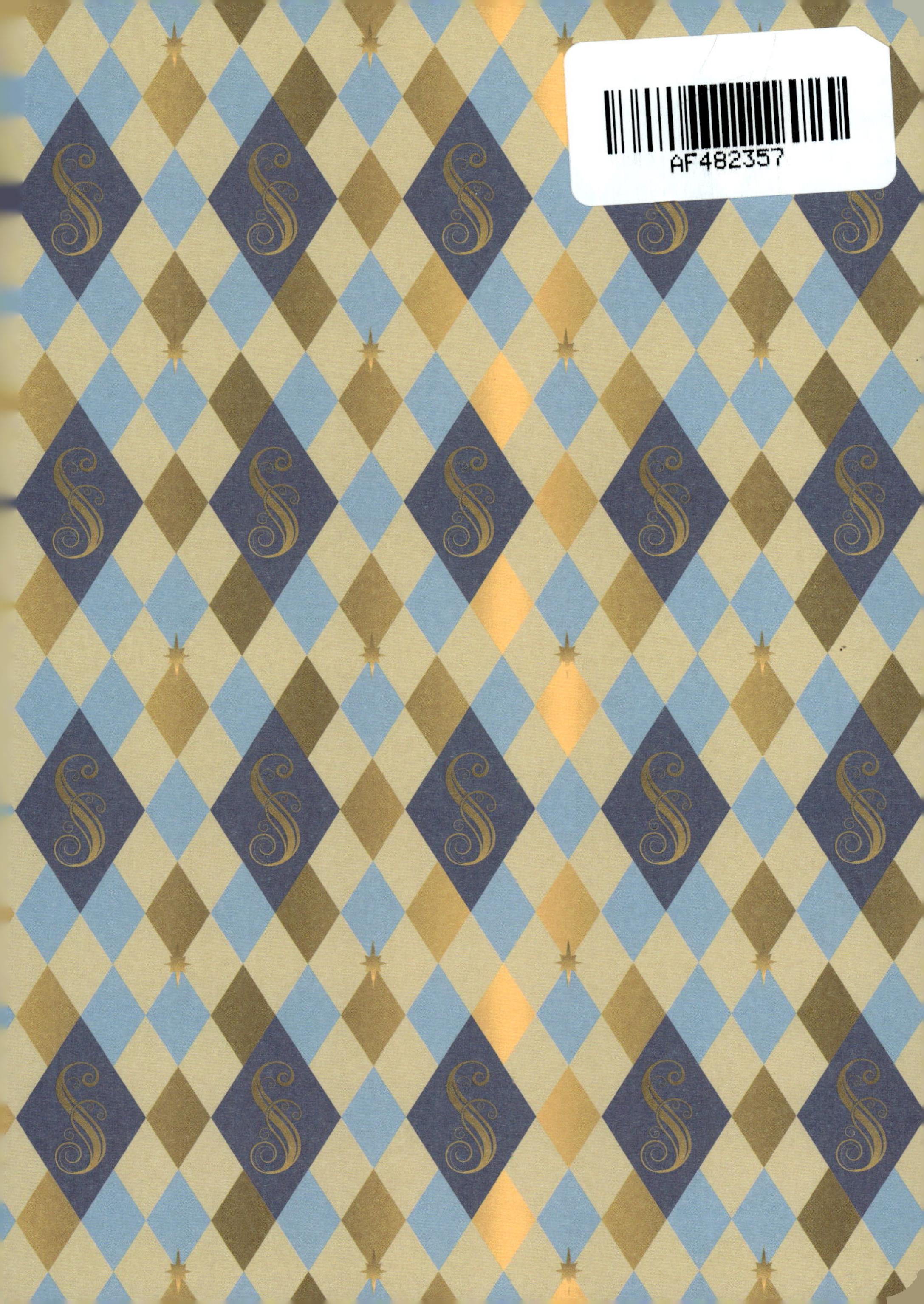

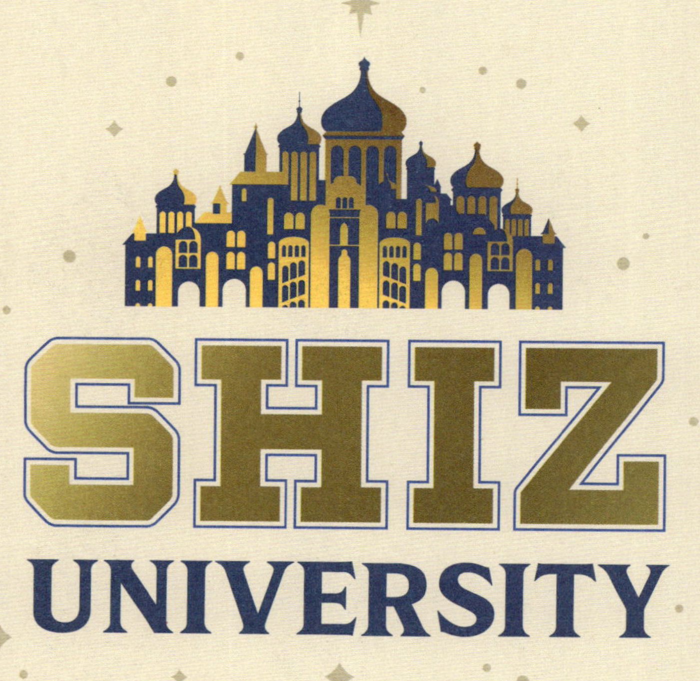

SHIZ
UNIVERSITY

THIS BELONGS TO

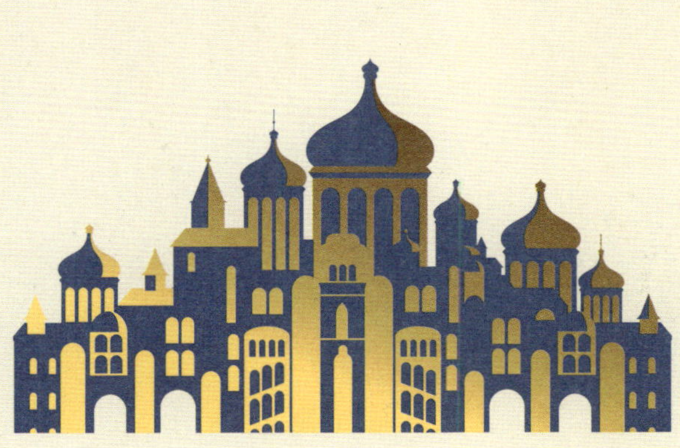

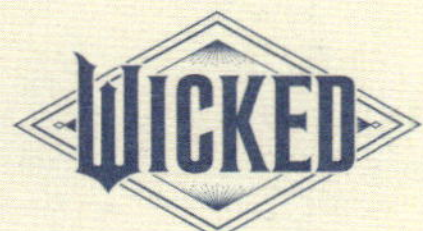

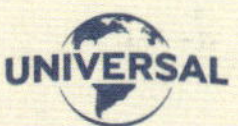

INSIGHTS

insighteditions.com

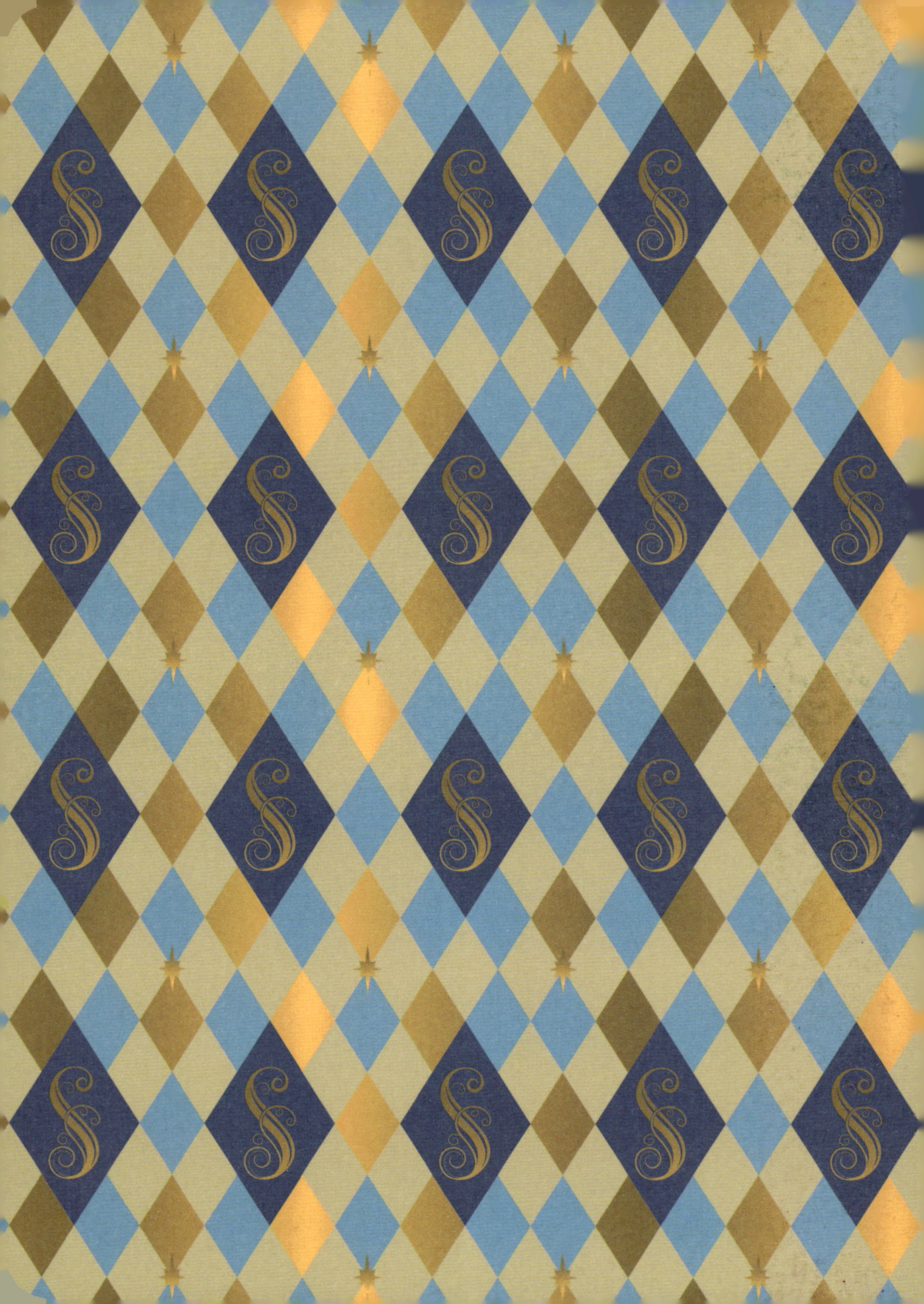